a love letter to her....

The bee sting

Her lips the taste of honey
And her eyes the color of the comb
And Her I love you's?
They're with a scent of gold

The way she loved indescribably great
But the way she hurt,
You can see she was carrying an abundance of pain
And in her smile she showed me her hate
But with her eyes she said this is our fate

I couldn't leave but I couldn't stay
Her mouth whispered pretty words that made me believe this is okay

**Drained.**

Eventually love won't be enough
So when you've given all you could give your left feeling drained

Drained

I can't seem to fall in love
When I think about love I think about her

The way her eyes shut when she laughed
Or the way her smile looked when she tried to be mad

I can't seem to forget the dimple on her left cheek
Or the way she looked when she was ready to eat

I can't picture myself with another human being
I refused to believe we aren't meant to be

Yet here we are

She was muse
But it's over now because she lit the fuse

Drained

When she tells me she loves me i don't believe it
How could you say those words and not mean it

To love and to be loved is such and undying feeling
Unless of course your tired of healing
And in that case your heart will start peeling

After its peeled and shattered apart
She will come back and you'll realize you weren't hers from the start

And in the end it's too late
Your heart is already filled with hate

I blame her for my current mental state.

Drained

I want you to love me the way you love coffee in the morning
I want you to see me the way you see a sunset

And I want you to hug me like it's the last hug you'll get

I don't want to be your crush I want to be your infatuation
I want the earth to revolve around us
I want us to evolve together

I can say I want it all but things won't ever change
Instead you love me the way you love brocoli

And you see me the way you see a willow tree

I'm not delusional I knew it would never be me
But part of me was hoping eventually it would be

Drained

Over Romanticizing myself is what I do best
Which is why It's hard to put my feelings to rest
You called it true love's test

And when I think I'm done
And these feelings are shunned
You call and I think "she must be the one"

I have a tendency to not put myself first
And when I do it makes me feel worse.

drained

If i stay a little longer
Then Maybe her heart will grow a little fonder

If I don't leave today
Then maybe this time she'll stay

If I don't indulge the fight
Then maybe we can make this right
Maybe this time I'll be her light

Drained

You sucked all the air from my lungs
while you said my name with your tongue

And truth be told you had nothing to offer
But my heart couldn't help but wander

I told you I had enough love for the both of us but when I said that I didn't want you to drain me of it.

Drained

Some days I wished I never met you
then I remember what we've been through

Eventually you'll disappear from my mind like flea but until then you'll still be taunting me in my head like a fever dream

Drained

She doesn't love me enough not to lie
And sometimes it makes me want to die

But she "loves" me

she acts like hanging out is a crime
It's no wonder why she's always low on time

Her actions always make me wonder why
I honestly think I'm done being the secret she desperately hides

Her name and the word narcissist fit together perfectly fine

drained

I just can't seem to fall in love
I can't seem to look at others the way they look at
Me

I can't feel the infatuation that I see

I have been in love once
And I don't think anyone else will be good enough

I want to feel the butterflies again
But it seems like my love life reached its end

**The realization.**

Eventually you will realize you weren't the problem they where
It's not that your love wasn't enough, you were just giving it to someone who couldn't accept it. You learn to realize that you are enough and the person you needed to love was yourself.

The realization

And in the end we wouldn't work
it's like my mind was stuck in a curse

I swore I would never do this again
But here i find myself bundled up in your bed

Although my heart still beats for you i'm beginning to think our love wasn't true

The realization

It didn't matter how much i loved her
She was to busy loving someone else

The realization

I believe i'm here to fix people
And when I fix them and they're eyes shine bright
They tend to thank me by leaving me in the night

I repaired her broken damaged soul
I was the reason she felt whole

And for my sake you said you'd stay
But here you are walking away

I repaired this home that I didn't break.
And You threw my heart aside like a rake.

The realization

I was warned not to pursue you
That made me want you even more

## The realization

I always knew you'd come back when you wanted to. I saw aside of you no one else understood. I made you feel loved and safe and I wish I could say I felt the same.

My home is no longer sane
my mind has been misplaced

And as I let you come in and out
I feel myself sinking above the ground

Staying put for you isn't ideal
You make me feel like life isn't real

I thought If love was easy it wasn't worth chasing
But now I'm filled with pain and a heart that won't stop aching

The chase was thrilling it gave me a rush
But when I said I loved her she told me to " hush"

I've said it so many times before
But if you didn't love me then why continue to knock on my door

I now know why I always felt unsure
Your Love isn't something i need to risk life for

The realization

we need to spend time apart
Staying together seems to only break our hearts
I'm tired of arguing
I'm tired of making up

It really hurts to say this but
I think it's time for us to actually break up

The realization

If i let you in again i know this time won't be different
I learned your pattern of hurt
So if i let you in this time will be worse
I've decided i have more self respect

The realization

You only decide to love me when no one else will
You only love me when you can't love yourself

The realization

You say part of your heart will always love me
But i don't deserve to be partially loved

So i'm dismissing the parts of me that longed for you

**Hypocrite.**

**It wouldn't be fair to assign you all the blame for it, I did something I wasn't proud of.
I never took it as far as you did but I know my words hurt.**

Hypocrite

I was more then broken
And for a while all i did was blame you
Then i realized there were days i treated you the same too
I wouldn't say it was to the same extent
But i know my words left your mind with dents

Hypocrite

It takes two to break a heart
And maybe mine wasn't the start

Insecurities had my mind in a chain
So maybe it was hard to rap your hurt around my brain

Is it possible her heart hurt the same
Was i the one who caused her pain

Hypocrite

I hid my heart with flames
And realized you didn't deserve all the blame

The love i had for you was insane
But sometimes i treated you inhumane

Hypocrite

I pushed her to stay
I couldn't stand the feeling of letting her walk away

So i didnt let her
And she resented me for it

Some of her actions were justifiable
Even if my feeling were undeniable

hypocrite

I wasn't what she needed
She knew it, i wouldn't accept it

**Storm within me.**

**Being with you felt like standing in front of a tornado,
you never know how much damage it will truly cause**

Storm with in me

The days we laughed until we couldn't breathe
Those are the days I wish I could repeat

Now the storms set everyday
I wish there was a way to get away

For every morning of laughter comes a week of tears
we tend take 1 step forward but 2 steps backwards

**Storm within me**

Sometimes I call you because it makes it all better
But then I remember you change like the weather

Storm within me

Some days my eyes would turn into storms
while yours would enrage in fire

And me calling out your name before the word liar

Yet I believed you.

I believed you when you said you would never do it again
I believed you when you said "oh dont worry shes just a friend"

I don't know why i'm so surprised, your mouth has always been filled with lies
So let the storm wash you away
Maybe then i can live a life without ache

Storm within me

Sometimes I call you because it makes it all better
But then I remember you change like the weather

Storm within me

My eyes water plants
No wonder why the rain got so envious

Storm within me

Thank you for loving me the way
Hurricanes love houses

**Healing.**

It took me reaching rock bottom to decide it's time for me to heal
In my opinion it's the most dreadful journey a person could go on. It's like recovery but for a hopeless romantic who can't stop loving. And The timeline for healing is never ending, you have to allow yourself to heal. The impatient will never heal, healing is a long process and it can't be rushed And I had to learn this the hard way. The process of healing wasn't easy, but I'm glad I did it. I now find comfort in my own skin.

Healing

I am more than my body
And more than a piece of skin
you seek refuge in

I am love
I am the feeling when the the
leaves turn yellow
I am the way the water taste
on a hot summer day
I am abundant
And your "love" in now
redundant

You couldn't love me for who I
was
And at times I thought "am I
not enough"

I've found the peace I'd been
looking for
And that means I'm not with
you anymore

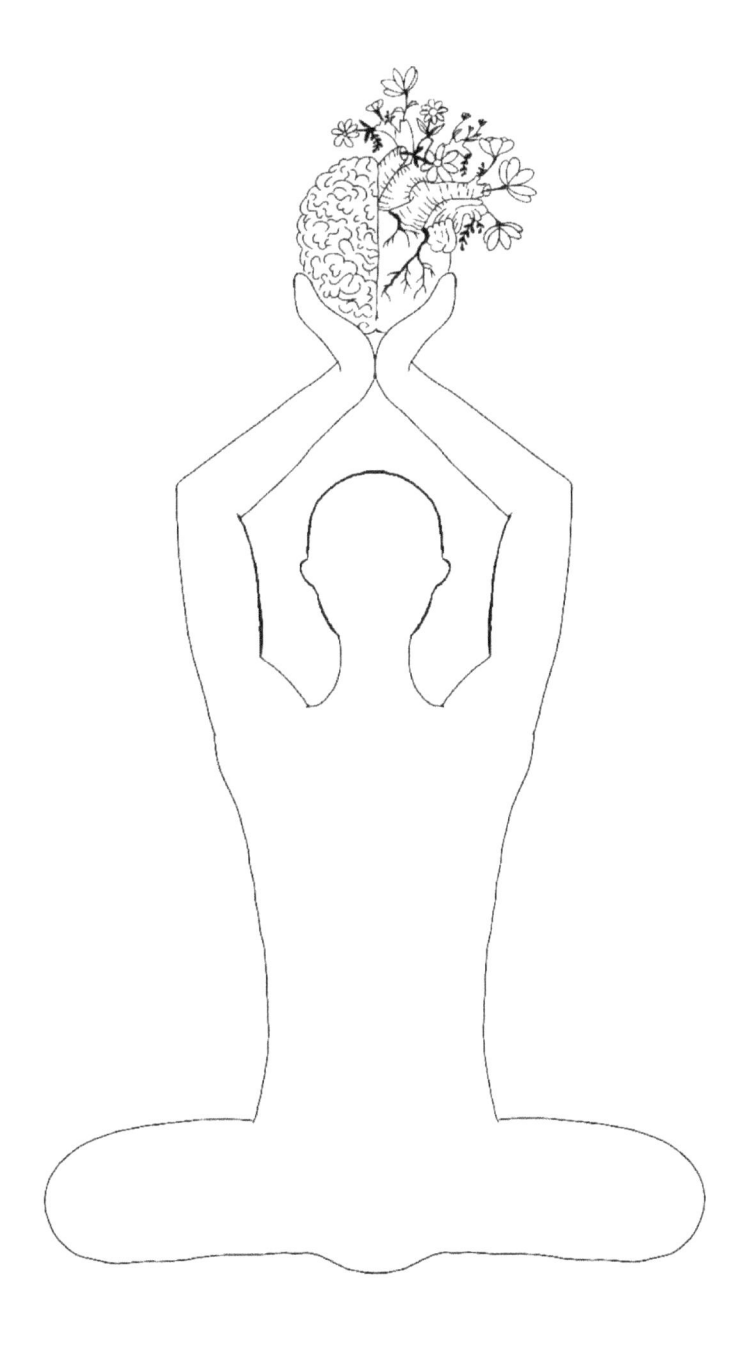

Healing

The sun will set and rise
Even if you aren't by my side
The earth will still rotate around the sun
Even if it's not us having all the fun
My world seems to have remained the same
While my mind has been driven mentally insane

The sun will never be as pretty as the day I met you
5 am comes and it's time to wake up and forget you
I live on this earth with my heart stuck in Neptune


I would have traded the sun for the moon if it meant I'd sleep next to you
I would have stopped the earth from turning if it meant I could stop all your hurting

But in the end it wasn't me
Now you live in my head rent free

Healing

One day I woke up and decided to let the chaos be
I realized through all this ache you'd never choose me

I knew that if I loved her more than I loved myself
I would never make it out alive

Healing

I lost interest the moment you started putting me last
Not to worry I've decided I'm leaving you in the past

Eventually the little things will get bigger
And I'm at a capacity with your bullshit

Healing

And if all I have left is this picture of us
then it's time to let the ashes burn and turn into dust
You've exploited my world long enough
It goes without saying the past three years had been rough

## Healing

I walked into our coffee shop the other day
Thinking our memories would just fade away

They didn't

Instead i saw you
In every sip of my coffee
In every person i passed
In every breathe i took

I saw you

As i left i waved goodbye
Goodbye to that memory
Goodbye to that coffee shop
Goodbye to you

And i know it seems harsh
Buts its the only way ill get over you

ill do what i can
To erase that memory

Keeping it wont make me a better me

## Healing

Maybe in another life we would have worked
And of course i said that and smirked

healing

The process of healing really hurt
I will no longer allow myself to be treated like dirt

## Healing

If I ever fall in love again
Let it be pure
Let it be so beautiful god herself couldn't describe it
Let it be genuine
Let it be filled with happiness
Let it be love
I hope that they're funny
I hope that they're sweet
And I really hope that the next girl can be apart of my peace
If I ever fall in love again let it be real

Healing

And so I had to learn to love myself
But that meant unloving you

I had to leave so I could heal
Even tho all of my feelings were still real

You called me selfish
But I knew you wouldn't understand
So that night I took the liberty and gave my heart
helping hand

I am no longer at your disposal
I am no longer waiting for your proposals
I had to leave to love myself

Happily ever after every girls dream
Not someone who makes them cry and scream

The illusionment these fairy tales told
Hey I mean at least the lies were sold

The truth is nothings what it really seems
A gray picture still has white lines in between

Your heart tells you to leave so you can get better
Notice how this isn't a love letter

**The end**

A love letter to her is a book I wrote in my college dorm room. I want to thank all of my best friends for encouraging me to write and publish this book. Thank you so much for the insane amount of love and support i love you all.

**Cover design and art work**

**By
Ella murphy**

CPSIA information can be obtained
at www.ICGtesting.com
Printed in the USA
LVHW021801200623
750236LV00009B/537